LIVING DANGEROUSLY

LIVING DANGEROUSLY

American Women Who Risked Their Lives for Adventure

by Doreen Rappaport

HarperCollins*Publishers*

For Thecla Mitchell

LIVING DANGEROUSLY:
American Women Who Risked
Their Lives for Adventure
Copyright © 1991 by Doreen Rappaport
All rights reserved. No part of this book may be
used or reproduced in any manner whatsoever without
written permission except in the case of brief quotations
embodied in critical articles and reviews. Printed in
the United States of America. For information address
HarperCollins Children's Books,
a division of HarperCollins Publishers,
10 East 53rd Street, New York, NY 10022.
Typography by Elynn Cohen
1   2   3   4   5   6   7   8   9   10
First Edition

Library of Congress Cataloging-in-Publication Data
Rappaport, Doreen.
  Living dangerously : American women who risked their lives for
adventure / Doreen Rappaport.
    p.   cm.
  Includes bibliographical references.
  Summary: Six stories of American women who defied social
convention to undertake dangerous adventures.
  ISBN 0-06-025108-5. — ISBN 0-06-025109-3 (lib. bdg.)
  1. Adventure and adventurers—United States—Juvenile literature.
2. Women—United States—Biography—Juvenile literature.
[1. Adventure and adventures.]   I. Title.
CT3260.R37   1991
973'.082—dc20   90-28915
[B]   CIP
[920]   AC

"Please know that I am quite aware of the hazards. I want to do it—— because I want to do it. Women must try to do things as men have tried. When they fail, their failures must be but a challenge for others."

—Amelia Earhart, American aviatrix
From a letter to her husband, George
Putnam, before her 1937 around-the-
world flight, during which she disappeared

🦋 ACKNOWLEDGMENTS 🦋

The following people generously shared their expertise in assuring the accuracy of details in these stories: Michael Adas, Rutgers University; Joe Daly; Russell Lee; Donald Loker, Local History Specialist, Niagara Falls Public Library; Elizabeth Fagg-Olds; Dominick Pisano, National Air and Space Museum; Patty Reilly-Butcher; Paddy Rossbach; Dwight Whalen; Terry Wilson.

Dick Traum, of the Achilles Track Club, provided a press pass so that I might be present at the start of the New York City Marathon.

Anne Emerman, Frieda Zames, Antoinette D'Orazzio and Paddy Rossbach led me to Thecla Mitchell. My special thanks to Eugenie Clark and Thecla Mitchell for sharing their lives. Linda Margolin and her fifth-grade class at P.S. 84 Manhattan generously critiqued "The Birthday Party." My continued appreciation to my editor, Katherine Brown Tegen, for pushing me to the limits.

❧ CONTENTS ❧

THE
BIRTHDAY PARTY

October 25, 1901
Niagara Falls, New York

"Mrs. Taylor, do you really think you're going to shoot the falls and live to talk about it?"

Annie Edson Taylor smoothed the front of her long skirt, adjusted the feather on her hat and smiled for the photographer. "Of course."

By tomorrow Annie would be famous. In newspapers all over the world people would read about the teacher who went over Niagara Falls in a barrel on her birthday and lived.

Niagara is only the forty-ninth highest falls in the world; but when measured in terms of the power and volume of the water flowing over, it is the third greatest waterfall in the world. Niagara Falls is really two waterfalls: the Horseshoe Falls on the Canadian side and the American Falls on the U.S. side. Annie was going over on the Canadian side, where the Niagara River thunders and foams and pounds as it drops 186 feet in one leap.

Annie wasn't the first person to defy death at the falls. Since the early 1800s daredevils had sought fame and fortune here. Sam Patch was the first. In 1829 Patch successfully jumped feetfirst from a 90-foot platform into a pool at the bottom of the American Falls, where the falls meet the lower river. In 1859 Jean Francois Gravelet, "The Great Blondin," walked on a tightrope across the Niagara gorge, a mile north of the falls. In 1876 Maria Speletrina became the first woman ever to walk a rope across the Gorge.

But some daredevils weren't as lucky. Matthew Webb managed to swim from the *Maid of the Mist* sightseeing boat landing on the Canadian side down the Niagara River, but drowned in the Whirlpool Rapids.

Only one person—a woman—had tried to go through the Niagara Rapids below the falls in a barrel. A month earlier spectators had watched, horrified and helpless, as Maud Willard's barrel swirled around and around for hours in the middle of Whirlpool Rapids. By the time her barrel was retrieved, Willard had suffocated to death from lack of air.

People predicted that if Annie didn't suffocate like Willard, her bones would be broken when the barrel split from the pounding of the water or from hitting rocks along the way. The chief of police on the New York State side of the falls was so sure she would kill herself that he had announced, "If I catch her, I'll arrest her for attempted suicide, and I'll arrest anyone who helps her." His words had scared off one man who had promised to help Annie.

Annie didn't feel scared, even though she knew how dangerous this stunt was. From the time she was little she had relished adventure. As a young girl she had preferred the outdoors to the indoors, sports to dolls, and tales of pirates and war to dull classroom readers. When her husband had died thirty years earlier, she'd left her family and friends in the East and had gone to teach in San Antonio, Texas. But the western frontier didn't quell her restless nature. She had kept on traveling. She'd gone south and taught dancing, calisthenics, and nutrition in Chattanooga, Tennessee; Asheville, North Carolina; and Birmingham, Alabama. She'd gone north to Washington, D.C., and west again to Chicago, Illinois, and finally to Bay City, Michigan.

Annie found adventure even when she didn't seek it. At a music recital in Charleston, South Carolina, she had found herself in the middle of an earthquake. More than 110 people died in the quake and hundreds more were injured, but Annie survived unharmed.

On a stagecoach trip in Texas she was held up at gunpoint. When a masked robber pressed a loaded pistol to her head and demanded her money, which she had hidden in the folds of her dress, she said, "Blow away.

I would as soon be without brains as without money." He backed off.

Adventure had enriched Annie's life, but it had not enriched her pocketbook. At sixty-three she was broke. So she was taking one last adventure, an adventure more daring than any she had ever read about. If she succeeded, she believed, she would become not only famous, but rich.

There was already great interest in her. Reporters had been following her for days. Over a thousand people were gathered at observation points along the way, eager for even a glimpse of her barrel on its journey.

"That's all for now, Mrs. Taylor," said the photographer.

Annie walked along the American shore to where the rowers were receiving last-minute instructions from Fred Truesdale. Truesdale was a skilled oarsman who knew the currents in the upper Niagara River well. He and his men would tow Annie's barrel to a place above the falls near the Canadian shore where the rapids were mostly unobstructed by rocks. He would release the barrel where the current would maximize Annie's chance of making it down the river and over the falls in one piece.

Truesdale rolled the barrel off the grass into the water. Annie had designed the four-and-a-half-foot oak barrel. A cooper in Michigan had made it to her specifications. The barrel was an unusual shape. The top was 36 inches in diameter, and it tapered to 15 inches at the bottom. Ten iron hoops were bolted around it at regular intervals. The barrel weighed 160 pounds—100 pounds of which was an anvil placed at the bottom to keep the barrel upright and to minimize Annie's battering by the current.

Truesdale rolled the barrel out of the water back onto the grass. He saw that water had seeped in. "A seam's opened," he told Annie. "Some wood must have contracted. Probably last night when it was on land." Annie watched impatiently as he plugged up the hole.

He turned to her. "We're ready now, if

you are," he said. She asked the men to walk away. She took off her hat, her jacket and her skirt. She knew most people would consider her petticoat improper public attire, but it was lightweight and practical. She unbuttoned her blue-and-white shirtwaist at the neck and crawled backward into the barrel.

It wasn't easy getting in. Annie weighed 160 pounds, and the opening was narrow. In addition, she had to slip into a harness. The harness had a belt that fit around her waist. It also had a strap that ran from the back of the belt down through an iron flange screwed to the floor of the barrel, and then back up to the front of the belt, where it was fastened with a buckle. The harness would keep her feet down and keep her from bouncing up and hitting the lid with her head.

Annie slipped her hands into two leather straps nailed tight to the barrel near her elbows. She crooked her arms upward, then rested her hands near her chin. Her head rested on a pillow, another precaution against butting her head. There were large cushions to protect both sides of her body from her shoulders to her knees.

"Come on back," she called when she was settled in.

The men rolled the barrel out into shallow water so photographs could be taken of Annie in it. Then it was lugged back onshore. Truesdale put on the cover, which had rubber around the rim for a watertight fit. It was

fastened by a heavy oak button that slipped around a screw.

Seconds after the cover was secured, Annie called out, "I see light." Her voice was muffled through the barrel. She tapped on the area near the leak. Truesdale plugged it up with a strip of cloth.

"Okay now?" he asked.

"Okay."

"We're going to pump the air in now."

The bicycle pump moved up and down as air entered through a rubber hose at the top of the barrel. Near Annie's mouth was a spout that was attached to the hose. She would cork it up to keep the air in.

"Got enough?" the men yelled after pumping for twenty minutes.

"I think so."

Two men rolled the barrel into the shallow water again.

"There's water in here," Annie shouted.

"Don't worry," said Truesdale. "You'll be over the falls in minutes, and the water will help keep the barrel up."

He fastened a small rope to screw eyes on either side of the lid of the barrel and tied the rope to his boat. Another cable was run from the second boat to the barrel.

"Let's go," he ordered.

A man waded into the water and pushed the barrel farther, into deeper water. It floated. The boats started rowing toward the Canadian shore, pulling Annie along with them. For a few minutes she drifted slowly in gentle waters. Then the current got swifter. A quarter mile from the rapids Truesdale saw that the current was strong enough to propel the barrel along. He yelled to the rowers in the other boat, "Pull away," and they cut the rope to the barrel. "I'm casting off," he shouted to Annie. His boat was dangerously near the head of the rapids. "Ready, Mrs. Taylor?"

"Ready."

He cut the rope and then rowed away as fast as he could. Suddenly the barrel was upright, its lower half submerged in the water. The anvil had pulled it down. The current quickened. The barrel bounced up and down, in and out of the water. Annie bounced with it, but the harness kept her stable.

The cold water coming into the barrel chilled her. Around, around, the barrel whirled about like a top. She grasped the handles tighter. It felt as if the belt wasn't holding her. The barrel hit some rocks. The cushions absorbed some of the shock, but the jolts worried her; she was afraid the barrel would be smashed to bits. The barrel whirled away from the rocks, then whirled back and hit more rocks, and more rocks. Annie prayed her head wouldn't hit the top of the barrel.

Faster, faster. The barrel gathered speed as it moved down the river. Annie didn't hear the shouting as people all along the shore watched the barrel bob up and down.

Within four minutes the barrel reached the top of the falls. It paused a second, as if making up its mind whether or not to go, and then it plunged into the foaming falls. The spectators raced along the precipice to find a spot to watch the barrel emerge from the churning waters. Suddenly it appeared, then disappeared quickly. Within seconds it appeared again. Then it was gone. The crowd's shouts were drowned out by the roar of the falls.

Up, down and around. Up, down and around. Again and again the barrel whirled with ferocious speed. The roar of the falls was deafening. Annie's head felt as if it were splitting apart. She grasped the handles tighter but felt herself losing her grip. Her heart was pounding so fast, she thought it would burst.

Up, down and around. Up, down and around. She felt the body harness loosening. Cold water ran down her head and shoulders. It felt good for a minute. But then there was more water, and more water, and her body started to feel numb. She closed her eyes and tightened her lips. *What if I swallow too much water and choke to death?* Up, down, around. Up, down, around. *If only I weren't so dizzy. If only* . . . The fierce momentum lurched her forward and she lost consciousness.

Seventeen minutes later the barrel emerged in an eddy near a huge rock about 500 yards from the foot of the falls. A man with a long hook snagged the barrel's towline and drew it in. Another man got into the water and grabbed the rope and passed it on to a third man. Slowly the men heaved the barrel out of the water onto a large rock. It was in one piece. They hurried to open it, wondering whether Annie was alive or dead.

When they got the lid off, Annie lifted her head weakly. "She's alive," one man shouted. The news was relayed to the spectators by a megaphone. On the shore hoorays and tumultuous applause congratulated Annie, but she was too weak to notice it.

The men knew Annie was in no condition to unfasten the harness herself. They tried to pull her out through the narrow opening, but it was impossible.

"Get me a saw," one man shouted. The implement appeared, and the man sawed a large opening. Two men lifted Annie out and placed her gently on a huge rock.

"Are you okay?" someone asked, staring at the cuts and bruises on her scalp. Annie nodded. The nod was so feeble, the man thought she was going to faint. But she didn't.

A boat was brought up to the rock, but the water was too choppy for it to get close enough to Annie. A wooden plank was placed across the water between the rock and the shore. "Think you can make it?" someone asked, helping her up. Annie nodded. Two men supported her from behind as she tottered across the plank. When she reached the other side, someone grabbed her and wrapped blankets around her. She was shaking from the cold.

The men helped her down the path to a boat. They rowed to a landing, where a carriage took her back to her lodgings on the American side.

A doctor examined Annie and dressed her scalp wound. She had a slight concussion and multiple bruises but no broken bones. The reporters pressed to interview her, and despite her condition, Annie agreed. All through the interview she was delirious, talking clearly one moment, babbling the next, then crying.

"It was a terrible nightmare, and I'd sooner be shot by a cannon or lose a million dollars than do it again," she said. "But I'm not sorry I did it if it helps me financially."

Annie became famous temporarily, but her dreams of fortune did not materialize. She died penniless in 1921. Citizens in Niagara raised money to bury her.

During her lifetime the truth about Annie's age never came out. She had told everyone she was forty-three years old because she didn't think people would believe that a sixty-three-year-old woman could be strong enough and brave enough to go over Niagara Falls in a barrel.

THE MOUNTAIN
THAT REFUSED
TO BE CLIMBED

Friday, August 28–
Saturday, September 5, 1908
Yungay, Peru

Annie Smith Peck pushed open the shutters and leaned out the window. She looked past the square in Yungay's center, down a narrow dirt road lined by red-roofed houses, past the fields of wheat and corn, up to the snow-capped twin peaks of Huascarán, the highest mountain in Peru. It was a maze of snow and ice at over 22,000 feet (6,700 meters) above sea level. No one had ever climbed it to the top.

Huascarán is shaped like a horse's saddle.

Thousands of feet of rocky slopes lead to an immense glacier that spans the twin peaks. The glacier is a moving mass of ice. Anyone climbing it may encounter dangerous crevasses—deep fissures that drop suddenly into abysses—and snow avalanches that unexpectedly thunder down.

Climate is another danger. Ice-cold winds batter the mountain. At such high altitudes there is less oxygen to breathe. The body's metabolism slows down. Every step tests a person's physical endurance to its limits. No wonder no one had ever reached the top.

In the last four years Annie had tried five times to scale these snowy peaks and icy crags, and five times she had failed. Her last attempt had been only ten days ago.

People constantly asked her why she pursued this dangerous, impossible dream. Annie didn't try to make them understand. She didn't think that people who viewed mountains from valleys or from railroad trains could ever understand the beauty and power of those white-domed peaks floating toward the deep blue of the sky, belonging more to heaven than to earth.

But it wasn't only the beauty of mountains that attracted Annie. Ever since childhood Annie had taken on challenges. As the youngest child and only girl among three brothers, she had learned not to be intimidated by men's supposedly superior physical strength and endurance. When her brothers refused to let her join them in their games, she practiced until she was as good as they were, if not better. When her brothers went off to college, Annie vowed she would go too, even though there were only a few women's colleges and fewer coed colleges at that time. In 1874 she gained admission to the University of Michigan. She majored in Greek and excelled in every subject she studied. But earning a college degree wasn't enough for Annie. She went on to get a master's in Greek and became one of the first women college professors in the United States.

In 1885, on a trip through Switzerland, Annie saw the 14,690 foot (4,478 meter) Matterhorn, and her passion for the classics started to give way to a passion for mountain climbing. She became determined to scale its "frowning walls." She prepared by climbing smaller mountains in Greece and Switzerland. In 1888 she and her oldest brother scaled California's 14,162 foot (4,316 meter) Mount Shasta. In 1895 she became the third woman to conquer the Matterhorn.

She became instantaneously famous. People marveled at the endurance and courage of this woman, forty-five years old and barely five feet tall. Her climbing outfit—a hip-length tunic, short pants, high boots and a canvas hat tied with a veil under her chin—created as much of a sensation as her daring achievement. How unladylike, men said, and many women agreed. But Annie refused to wear floor-length skirts like other women climbers. It was ridiculous and dangerous to dress "like a lady."

Annie's triumph over the Matterhorn propelled her on. She gave up teaching and became a full-time climber, supporting herself

MISS ANNIE S. PECK, A.M.

THE WORLD-FAMOUS MOUNTAIN CLIMBER, LECTURER, AND WRITER, OFFICIAL DELEGATE OF THE UNITED STATES TO THE INTERNATIONAL CONGRESS OF ALPINISTS, 1900, PRESENTS THE FOLLOWING LECTURES

Each Illustrated by 100 or more Wonderful Views which cannot be Duplicated in this Country. The Lectures may also be given without Illustrations

Bolivia and Mt. Sorata

Peru and Mt. Huascaran
See Harper's Dec. 1906
Panama and the Canal

Mexico, with Ascents of Popocatepetl and Orizaba

The Passion Plays of Europe

Also

Business Opportunities in South America and the Pan American Railway.

To the Summit of the Matterhorn

Afoot and Alone in Tyrol

Switzerland, with Ascent of the Jungfrau

Athens, The Acropolis, and Ten other Lectures on Greece

MISS PECK IN CLIMBING COSTUME

Holding a second degree from the University of Michigan, the first woman to study at the American School of Archæology in Athens, having occupied the Chair of Latin at Purdue University and Smith College, Miss Peck is called by competent judges one of the most scholarly and accomplished women in the United States. Practically single-handed and alone she has accomplished extraordinary tasks. She has ascended higher on this hemisphere than any other American man or woman—to a height of approximately 20,500 feet on Mt. Sorata, in Bolivia—while in Peru she has made one first ascent and explored a section of country practically unknown here.

Miss Peck may be addressed at Hotel Albert, New York

• 21 •

by lecturing about her adventures. By 1900, having achieved over twenty successful climbs, she was recognized as one of the world's foremost climbers in a field still considered a man's sport.

But that wasn't enough for Annie either. She became determined to conquer a mountain no man had ever conquered. That mountain was Huascarán.

Annie closed the shutters, picked up her clothing sack and a heavy wool poncho and went downstairs. The four porters were carrying the expedition equipment outside. One sack held the ice axes, climbing irons, poles and ropes. Annie's lightweight silk tent and the sleeping bags were rolled up in the corner. The kerosene stove and kettles filled a third sack. Food was in a fourth bag. In a fifth bag were Annie's camera and a hypsometer, which she would use to measure the altitude at the top of Huascarán to establish its exact height.

Annie gave her clothing and poncho to one of the men. As temperatures dropped on the climb, she would eventually wear everything in the sack: two woolen face masks, fur mittens, black woolen sleeves, three suits of lightweight wool underwear, two pairs of tights, two pairs of woolen stockings, knickers, two flannel shirts, a jacket and two sweaters. Her hiking boots were big and clumsy. They had to be four sizes larger than her regular shoes to accommodate the heavy stockings.

Unfortunately none of her clothing was water- or windproof. Admiral Peary, the famous Arctic explorer, had lent her a waterproof Eskimo suit, but on her last climb it had fallen irretrievably out of a porter's hands into a crevasse.

She went outside. Her guides, Gabriel Zumtaugwald and Rudolf Taugwalder, were supervising the packing of supplies on the horses. Like other expert climbers, Annie favored Swiss guides. They knew so much about snow and rock that they always chose the most practical and safe paths even when in unfamiliar territory.

Gabriel and Rudolf were skilled but stubborn, and impatient whenever Annie made suggestions—even though she was their employer and knew the mountain better than they did. They wouldn't listen when she suggested they wear at least two pairs of wool stockings. Her guides of two years ago, wearing two pairs of stockings, had barely escaped losing their toes to frostbite. They didn't like taking advice from a woman.

The party set off on horseback for the three-hour ride to the copper mines, where they would rest overnight before hiking to the snow line. The horses trotted down the narrow walled road out of the village and soon ascended to where the houses became more scattered. The air was fragrant with blossoms of yellow broom and blue larkspur. Fields of wheat and corn blanketed the landscape with deep yellows. On the mountain snow was falling. An occasional villager, bent from years of working in the fields, passed them on the road.

When they arrived at the mines, Annie felt faint and a bit sick. She didn't know why. The ride had been easy enough. She ate a small bowl of soup and two boiled eggs and lay down to take a nap. But sleep did not come easily.

When Annie saw clouds over the mountain the next morning, she postponed the ascent. The fresh snow needed at least another day of melting by the sun and freezing at night to make the mountain suitable for climbing.

At eight A.M. the next day they set out for the snow line. The walking was easy. Within six hours, they reached the first campsite, set up their tents, had soup and tea, and went to bed at sunset.

By seven the following morning they were at the glacier. The porters put climbing irons over their shoes to bite into the surface of snow and ice. Annie and the guides wore boots studded with nails. Annie's studs weren't as pointed as her guides', but she didn't want to wear climbing irons. On the last ascent the strap on one of Annie's irons had been too tight. It had hindered her circulation. Two of her toes and the top of her right foot had gotten slightly frostbitten.

The climbing continued to be easy. Annie's

instinct to wait the extra day had been right. The snow was easy to walk on. In seven hours they were well up in the saddle of the mountain. They pitched their tent under a snow wall. But despite the wall's shelter, a chilling wind swept through the tent all night.

There was no wind the next morning, but the air was thin and bitter cold. Annie thought it was the coldest day she had ever experienced on the mountain in all her climbs.

The ascent became radically steeper. Gabriel went first, probing for crevasses with his pickaxe and cutting small zigzag steps up the almost perpendicular wall. Annie, tied to a rope with Rudolf and a porter named Lucas, followed, pushing her pole into the glassy surface. The pole's pointed iron provided leverage, but the climbing was difficult and exhausting.

An hour later they reached a bridge of ice over a crevasse. Annie hesitated to cross it because there was no way to tell how strong it was. Rudolf crawled quickly over it on his hands and knees, then sat on the other side and wound the rope, still tied to Annie and the porter, around his ice axe to anchor it. Annie hurried across next, then knotted her length of rope around her ice axe. Lucas was carrying too much on his back to hurry across. He stepped cautiously onto the ice bridge and suddenly slipped off the bridge and disappeared into the crevasse. Annie heard his cry as she gripped the rope more firmly to keep from being pulled over with him.

"Quick, quick." Gabriel, tied to the other three porters on a second rope, motioned for the porters to untie themselves. He threw their rope down to Lucas, who—though hanging head down—managed to tie it to his own rope and miraculously turn himself upright. He tugged on the rope. Annie and the men pulled him up. Annie was relieved to see him, but was dismayed to see that his pack, with the new stove in it, was not with him. They couldn't go on without the stove.

"I'll go down for it," Gabriel said, and within seconds he was lowered down on a rope. Annie was worried. They were at least

19,000 feet above sea level. Exerting oneself at this height was dangerous. And maybe it was a fool's errand. There was no telling how deep the crevasse was or if Gabriel could even find the pack.

She waited impatiently. Ten minutes later Gabriel pulled on the rope. They hauled him up. The pack, with the stove in it, was in his hands.

They moved on. By dark they were at the top of the saddle. Tomorrow, with any luck, she would reach the top. *Finally, after all these years.*

Winds battered the tent all night and were so fierce the next morning that Annie suggested postponing the final climb until the wind died down.

"It's too dangerous," she said, "and we need rest." She was exhausted from the last two days and knew that the men had to be too, even though they wouldn't admit it.

"It'll be less windy higher up," countered Rudolf.

"I know this mountain," Annie argued.

"Unless the wind dies down altogether, it'll be worse higher up."

"I think Rudolf's right," said Gabriel. "We should go on."

Annie yielded reluctantly. They agreed to leave the porters behind.

She was wearing every stitch of clothing she had packed but the poncho. She didn't want to put it on yet. It was too clumsy. She slipped a mask over her face and neck and put on her fur mittens. Rudolf put on his face mask. Gabriel didn't have a mask. Annie offered him her extra one and was surprised when he graciously accepted it.

"Could one of you carry my poncho?" This was asking a big favor, for at this altitude every extra bit of weight was a strain.

Rudolf acted as if he didn't hear her. "I'll do it," said Gabriel, even though he was already burdened with the food sack and the bag with hypsometer and camera.

Within an hour of climbing the sun was higher in the sky and Annie's hands were sweating inside the fur mittens. She took off her fur mittens and exchanged them for two pairs of woolen mittens in Rudolf's sack. One pair did not cover the fingers.

Up, up, the climbing was slow and strenuous. The cold winds had blown away the lighter snow on the surface, and the glacier was like glass.

"I've never seen such large patches of ice on any mountain in Switzerland," Rudolf said.

"I told you Huascarán is the fiercest mountain in the world," Annie said proudly.

They turned a ridge, and the wind knifed through Annie. She took her poncho from Gabriel. She needed her fur mittens. They stopped, and Rudolf opened his sack.

"Which ones first?" he asked, tucking Annie's wool sleeves and fur mittens under his right arm.

Hold on to them tight, Annie thought, but she didn't say it.

"The sleeves."

Rudolf reached under his arm, but the wind got there first. Annie watched a fur mitten blow over the precipice. She was furious.

There was no way to retrieve it. The woolen gloves would never be warm enough, and now her hands would probably get frostbitten.

Rudolf apologized. Annie ignored the apology. She hastily put the one fur mitten on over the other gloves on her right hand, which carried her pickaxe. It was more exposed to the cold than the left hand.

Up, up. The air was so thin, Annie had trouble breathing. It became harder and harder to move her legs. It was even hard pushing the pickaxe into the icy surface.

They stopped to eat. The meat and bread had frozen in the sack, but it didn't matter. They were too tired to eat much anyway. They nibbled on chocolate and raisins and drank the partially frozen tea in Rudolf's canteen.

"I'm too tired to go any farther," Rudolf announced.

Annie didn't want to stop. They were probably only an hour away from the top. *So close now!* "You can rest and we'll go ahead," she said to Rudolf.

"No, let's all rest for an hour and then go

on," said Gabriel. Annie agreed reluctantly.

The hour's rest did little to revive them. When they started climbing again, the cold, thin air was so debilitating that they had to stop frequently.

At three P.M. they rounded the final rise leading to the top of the mountain. The wind was stronger than ever. Annie's left hand felt numb. She pulled off her mitten and saw that the hand was nearly black. She rubbed her fingers vigorously with snow to revive the circulation. The rubbing made her fingers ache, a good sign that they weren't frostbitten. She tucked her hands inside the poncho, grateful for its length.

"We'd better measure the altitude now," said Gabriel. "It may be too windy at the top."

They untied themselves from each other. Rudolf wandered off, but Annie paid no attention. She was too busy shielding the hypsometer from the wind as Gabriel struck one match after another, hoping to light the candles so they could boil the water. A hypsometer is an instrument that is able to determine altitude in relation to the boiling point of water, which decreases as altitude increases. Annie wanted to know exactly how high she was and whether she had set a world's record.

She looked around for Rudolf. *Where is he? Maybe if he helped, we could get the candles lit.* After twenty tries, they gave up. Annie was disappointed. Now she could only estimate how high the mountain really was.

"We'd better move on to the top. It's half past three," said Gabriel.

Annie looked around for Rudolf again.

Suddenly he appeared. "I've been to the top," he said.

How dare he steal the honor? He wouldn't have dared do this if I were a man. Just an hour ago he wanted to quit. And he hasn't done half as much work as Gabriel. The guides knew she expected, as was the tradition, that as organizer of the expedition she would be the first to place her foot on the top of the mountain.

I won't tell him now how mad I am, but if we get down alive, I'll tell him. If we get down alive . . . The thought frightened her.

She set out for the top without a word. The winds battered her, and several times she had to stop and lean on her pickaxe to catch her breath.

"Don't go too near the edge," warned Gabriel, stepping aside to let her arrive first on the top of the mountain.

I'm here after all these years. She wanted to shout for joy, but there was no time to waste. Soon it would be dark. It had taken seven hours to climb to the top. How long would it take to go down? Steep rocks and icy slopes were far more dangerous to descend than to climb. She hurriedly photographed the views on all sides.

They tied themselves together again. Rudolf led, cutting the steps. Annie was in the middle, Gabriel at the rear. Their lives depended on Gabriel. If they slipped and he couldn't hold the rope to stop their fall, all three could plunge to death.

They turned a ridge and confronted a sixty-degree slope. "Be careful," said Gabriel.

Something black flew by.

"What is it?" Annie cried.

"One of my mittens," said Rudolf. "I took it off to fasten my shoe."

Rudolf worked fast, cutting the steps the size of toeholds. Small steps were fine going up, but dangerous going down. Annie zigzagged her way down the steep slope. There was nothing to hold on to. She wished she had her climbing irons now. She needed that kind of grip on this glassy surface.

She missed a step and slid three feet. Gabriel's strong hands held the rope tightly, and she regained her footing. A few seconds later she missed another step and slipped again. She was about to yell, "It's not serious," when she slid again. Five, ten, fifteen feet down the incline. Again Gabriel's strong hands checked her fall.

"Get up," he yelled, but the rope was twisted so tightly around her waist that she couldn't move. The men came to her and hauled her up.

They moved on. Her poncho, swaying wide in the wind, constantly hid her view of her next step. Down, down she stepped. Again she slipped. Her fall pulled Rudolf down, too. Gabriel's strong hands checked both their falls.

I don't think we'll make it down alive. It's too dark and too slippery. And I'm so tired.

She slid again and again. She tried to convince herself that they would make it down alive.

She lost track of how much time was passing as she concentrated on each step. She wasn't even aware, three hours later, that they were on the gentler slope just over the campsite until Gabriel shouted, "We're safe. Now you can slide if you like."

Annie laughed. They untied themselves from each other and dragged their tired bodies toward the tent. It was half past ten. They were too tired to eat and almost too tired to lie down. But safety felt good.

In the tent Annie noticed both of Rudolf's hands were black. "Rub them hard," she said. But Rudolf was so weak, he couldn't do it. *I'll do it,* thought Annie, but she was too tired to do it. *I'll get a porter to do it.* But in her tiredness, she forgot.

The three climbers huddled together on one side of the tent across from the porters. Annie wrapped the blankets around herself and the two men. When she realized the middle was the warmest spot, she moved to the outside and let Rudolf be in the center.

When they awakened the next morning, the wind was fierce. They were too exhausted to complete the rest of trip down the mountain. By Thursday the wind had abated, and feeling more rested, they started down the mountain. They arrived at the mine two days later, on Saturday morning, September 5, about 10 A.M. After breakfast, they returned to Yungay.

Becoming the first person to climb to the top of Huascarán brought Annie world fame. The Peruvian government gave her a gold medal. In 1928 the Lima Geographical Society named the north peak of Huascarán Ana Peck. But Annie's triumph over Huascarán was marred for her by the subsequent amputation of Rudolf's left hand, a finger of his right hand and half of one foot.

Because the hypsometer had not worked, Annie

could only estimate Huascarán's height. At the saddle she and her guides had measured the altitude at 20,000 feet (6,100 meters). Based on this figure, they estimated that the north and south peaks were at least 23,000 feet (7,000 meters), making Huascarán the highest mountain in Peru and the highest mountain ever scaled by a man or woman.

Fanny Bullock Workman, up to this time the world's highest woman climber, challenged Annie's estimate of Huascarán. Bullock Workman sent a team of scientists to Yungay to measure Huascarán by triangulation: This method uses trigonometry to measure height. Bullock Workman's team concluded that the north and south peaks were no more than 21,812 feet (6,648 meters) and 22,187 feet (6,763 meters) respectively.

Annie eventually conceded that Huascarán was "not so lofty" as she had hoped. Bullock Workman still held the world's altitude record for a woman climber, but Annie had succeeded in climbing a mountain that no man or woman had ever climbed. Annie continued climbing until she was eighty-two years old.

BIRD-IN-FLIGHT

Waxahachie, Texas
Autumn 1923

Bessie Coleman stood with her arms folded tightly across her chest. "Sorry, but those are my terms. Either my people go in the same gate as the white people or I cancel the exhibition." Bessie tapped her right foot on the ground and stared over the heads of the two white men at the empty grandstand in Waxahachie, Texas. She could feel their anger even though she wasn't looking at them.

"Are you crazy?" the taller man shouted at her.

"What's the point?" the other man sneered. "Once they get inside, they're gonna sit separate anyway."

Bessie didn't answer. The thirty-year-old pilot didn't intend to lecture these men on the evils of segregation. She knew she had no chance of making them see her viewpoint. Nor did she have a chance of changing the rules that blacks and whites sat separately in public places. But she drew the line at the humiliation of her people entering by a different gate.

The men stomped away to talk. Out of the corner of her eye she followed their angry gestures as they argued back and forth about what to do. She was positive they were trying to decide if she was bluffing. She wasn't, but she sure hoped they'd give in. She desperately needed the money from this exhibition. But desperate as she was, she wouldn't budge an inch.

She glanced at her watch. Within minutes the gates would open. A large crowd was expected. Bessie was a curiosity, and everybody in and around Waxahachie wanted to see her. She was the local woman who had become the first licensed black pilot in the world.

Bessie's parents had left Oklahoma Territory when she was a baby, and settled in Waxahachie, about thirty miles south of Dallas. They bought a quarter acre of land and built a house. After ten years her father, who was part black and part Indian, decided to return to Oklahoma. Mrs. Coleman refused to go with him. She found work in Waxahachie as a laundress, but her meager earnings barely supported her five children. So every harvest Bessie and her siblings picked cotton to supplement their mother's wages. When Bessie got older, she helped with the washing and ironing.

Bessie's mother couldn't read or write, but she encouraged her children to read and to do well in school. She put aside money to rent them books from the wagon library that came to town twice a year. When Bessie was in high school, she decided she wanted to go to college. Her mother let her save the money she earned washing and ironing for the tuition. Bessie saved enough for one term at college. When she couldn't find a way to pay the next semester, she went to Chicago, where her brother lived, hoping to find a better job than picking cotton. She studied to be a manicurist and found a good job at a barber shop.

When she was twenty-eight, the flying bug hit Bessie. She read everything she could find about flying and decided she had to learn to fly. But where and how? Flying was still considered men's work. There were only a few women pilots. In 1910 Blanche Stuart Scott was the first woman to make a solo flight. For the next six years she did stunt flying and thrilled her audiences with her "death dive," a perpendicular plunge from 4,000 feet above the ground. Harriet Quimby, the first licensed woman pilot in the United States, received world recognition when she flew across the English Channel from Dover, England, to Calais, France, in 1912. Less than three months later she was killed in an exhibition in Boston.

Bessie knew that flying was dangerous and

that women fliers weren't taken seriously, but that wasn't going to stop her. She applied to aviation school, but no school in the United States would accept her because she was a woman and black.

She turned for help to Robert S. Abbott, founder of the black newspaper *Chicago Defender* and a known flight enthusiast. Abbott was moved by her determination. He suggested she learn French and go to study in France. Her family and friends tried to discourage her from going abroad, but Bessie stood firm and went. A year ago she returned home as the world's first black licensed pilot. She had been giving exhibitions ever since.

The two men walked hurriedly back toward her. "All right," the taller one said, not looking directly at her. "But they don't sit together."

She suppressed a smile and walked across the field toward an aisle out of view of the grandstand. It was a minor victory, but she felt good.

She felt even better when she saw the large

numbers of black people coming to the exhibition. Bessie wanted to encourage young black men and women to become pilots. She believed the airplane would revolutionize the future, and she wanted her people to be part of this dynamic change. That's why she had become a "barnstormer," one of those daredevils going from town to town giving exhibitions and taking people up for rides. Like these enthusiasts, she had bought a surplus army plane from World War I. She flew her Jenny from small town to small town giving exhibitions. She planned to use the money she earned as a stunt pilot to set up an aviation school for black Americans.

It was only twenty years since the Wright Brothers had flown at Kitty Hawk. The airplane was still considered magic—and dangerous. Stunt-flying accidents often headlined the news. But most Americans thought the risks were thrilling, and they gladly plunked money down to see acrobatic tricks in the air.

The applause started building as Bessie walked to the center of the field. The autumn heat was stifling. She was uncomfortably warm in her high boots, long jacket and pants, but she knew the audience expected her to wear such an outfit, and so she did. It was all part of a good performance.

When she reached the plane, she turned and acknowledged the applause by bowing. She jumped up on the wing, stepped into the cockpit and strapped herself in. After lowering her goggles over her eyes, she signaled the man at the propeller. He gave it a hard, quick turn. The engine started. Bessie waved to him, and he started walking away from the plane. A second man pulled the chocks, the blocks of wood that had held the plane stationary, away from the front and back of the wheels. The Jenny didn't have brakes. Bessie waved her hand back and forth, and the second man walked hurriedly away from the plane.

With a smooth, steady motion, she opened the throttle a bit and the engine started warming up. She opened the throttle wider. The engine roared and the airplane started rolling. Faster and faster. Two hundred feet, three hundred feet.

The plane began swinging side to side. The right wing tip almost scraped the ground. Suddenly the plane jerked up. It was a few feet off the ground. It was down. It leaned on one wheel, then on another. Now airborne, Bessie turned the plane and circled the perimeter of the airfield, then headed straight across the field. Faster and faster, toward the first row of the grandstand.

The motor roared. The plane was moving directly toward the grandstand. Spectators began screaming and ducking under their seats. In seconds the plane would crash into them. The propeller was almost touching the first row. A few people frantically climbed over seats to get out of the plane's way.

Suddenly the plane shot up into the air. The crowd roared with applause. Bessie climbed to 1,000 feet. The plane swung around, making a 180-degree turn and heading straight down toward the grandstand again. People started screaming again. The screams got louder and louder. Just at the moment it seemed that Bessie would crash into the grandstand, the plane swooped into the air again. The audience shrieked with delight.

Bessie flew higher and higher. The plane climbed 200 feet a minute. When she reached 1,500 feet, she swung the plane around and made another horizontal turn and began descending. She closed the throttle. The nose of the plane aimed at the ground. Down, down: 1,000 feet; 800 feet. She was gaining speed. The audience thought she had lost control; 500 feet, 300, 100. It looked as if in seconds she would crash.

She applied power and pulled the control stick back, and the plane shot up again. The applause was thunderous. But Bessie knew there was no time to relish it. The whole trick of stunt flying was to keep the audience on edge.

She flew up again. At 3,000 feet she pulled back the stick and applied right rudder. The nose came up, up, and the plane's climbing speed dropped rapidly. With a shudder, the Jenny stopped moving and seemed to hang in the air for a moment before the nose came down fast and the plane began spinning toward the ground like a corkscrew. With each turn Bessie lost 400 feet. She held the rudder and control stick hard in position. She was within 1,000 feet of the ground—600—500. She pushed the stick forward hard and straightened out the rudder to level off out of the spin.

Then she applied full power, pulled the stick back; the plane zoomed up into the air again. When she reached 3,000 feet, the plane spun down toward the ground again.

She started climbing once more, preparing for a set of slow loops. Audiences loved the long, slow motions of these large circles as the pilot looped back and forth. When she gained enough speed, she pulled the control stick back and the plane went into a steep climb. One thousand feet up she was at the top of the loop. Audiences loved this moment when the plane seemed to hang just before it dived down into a graceful circle.

She opened the throttle wide and pulled the stick back hard. Suddenly the motor went dead, and instead of a graceful circle, the plane started nosing down. This wasn't part of the routine. Bessie was dropping fast, without control. Her heart sank. Her breath came in short gasps. She wanted to swallow, but her mouth was too dry. She didn't know if she'd be able to land safely. Landing was always difficult in a Jenny even under the best conditions.

Don't panic, she told herself. She needed to keep a clear head, to use her skill to salvage the landing if she could.

When she was two hundred feet above the ground, she pushed the stick forward. She looked at the airspeed indicator. She was coming in "way too hot."

Fifty feet down. Thirty. Twenty. *Easy does it.* She pulled back the stick to level out the plane. *Easy does it.* The plane was parallel to the ground. The main wheels, then the tail gear touched the ground. *Easy . . . easy.* She looked across the field. It looked like she had at least 1,000 feet to slow down—plenty of room. The airplane rolled 800 feet to a quick stop. Bessie sighed with relief.

The audience screamed their approval, thinking it was part of the stunt. A few spectators jumped over the grandstand rail and ran toward Bessie. More people followed. Bessie jumped out of the cockpit.

"Please stay back," a man shouted to the crowd as he tried to put the chocks back under the wheels of the plane.

A nine-year-old boy pushed his way through the crowd to Bessie. "Lady, was your plane supposed to stop up there like that?"

Bessie laughed. "No, it wasn't."

Bessie continued giving flying exhibitions to raise money for her school. In 1924 at a show in California her plane crashed shortly after taking off. She broke several ribs and a leg. Her injuries did not discourage her, but her inability to raise money and realize her dream plagued her. On May 1, 1926, the local Negro Welfare Fund in Jacksonville, Florida, sponsored a show. She felt hopeful that some prominent wealthy blacks would attend the exhibition and be convinced to support her school.

On a practice run the night before, she was pulling out of a nose dive when her plane somersaulted.

Bessie fell 2,000 feet to her death. For some unex-plained reason, that day she had not strapped herself in or worn a parachute. Her mechanic, William Wills, also died when the plane crashed. It was later dis-covered that a wrench had slipped between the control gears and jammed them.

A letter from a twelve-year-old girl was found in Bessie's pocket. The girl wrote: "I am writing you to congratulate you on your brave doings. I want to be an aviatrix when I get [to be] a woman. I like to see our race do brave things. I am going to be out there to see you jump from the airplane. I want an airplane of my own when I get [to be] a woman. . . ."

THE HUNT

April 1925
Belgian Congo

It was six o'clock in the morning. The village was deserted. Delia Akeley was baking bread in a pan set on stones over a fire. Two women sat talking in front of a thatch-roofed hut, their babies on their laps. A man was teaching two boys how to throw a spear. Delia had no idea where the other villagers were. She lifted the cover of the pan and took out the bread to cool. No one paid attention to her.

Delia laughed, remembering what people had said when the Brooklyn Museum had announced that she was leading a safari across central Africa into the remote regions of the northeastern part of Belgian Congo, now the country of Zaire. This part of Africa was still a wilderness and relatively undisturbed by Westerners. Most Africans living here had never met a white man, and surely had never met a white woman. People told her it was too dangerous for a woman to travel through Africa with only African porters. They warned her to get an armed male escort. People just couldn't believe that a fifty-year-old woman—or any woman—was an accomplished hunter and capable of leading a safari in Africa. Delia had been concerned about the loneliness and isolation of the journey, but she had never once worried that she would be in any physical danger from the African peoples. And she had been proven right.

This was Delia's third trip to Africa. In 1905–6 and in 1909–11 she had come with her husband, Carl Akeley, to collect animal specimens for the American Museum of Natural History. Akeley was a taxidermist and

sculptor who had transformed the look of museum displays. Instead of just stuffing the preserved animal skins with soft material, Akeley mounted the skins over forms molded to the muscular contours of the animal's anatomy. Sometimes even museum experts thought his specimens were alive. Delia assisted him in reproducing the natural environments for the animal specimens. She photographed foliage, then painstakingly reproduced models. Her finished pieces showed every tiny detail in a leaf or bud or bush.

On the first safari, though she had never held a rifle in her hands, she had shot two elephants in the first week. Neither Delia nor her husband hunted for sport. She regretted killing any animal except for food or science. Delia thought it essential that Americans see the beauty and majesty of African wildlife, which she feared was fast being destroyed by white hunters and settlers. One of her elephants was displayed in Chicago's Field Museum.

On the second safari, her husband was attacked by an elephant while away from the main camp. Not knowing whether he was alive or dead, or even where he was, she rallied twenty men for a rescue party. They trekked through the forest, across canyons and over trails laced with traps laden with poisoned spears hung from trees. When she found Akeley, he was bleeding profusely. His nose was smashed, his ribs were broken and a lung was punctured. For the next three months he convalesced and she ran the safari. She nursed him, hunted for food and supervised the men. She began studying the animal life around her, particularly the primates.

Delia and Carl were divorced now, but her experience on the two safaris qualified her to be the first woman leading an expedition sponsored by a museum. On this trip she had traveled by foot and canoe through swamps and mud and jungle, the moisture-laden air so thick that her nostrils became clogged with wetness. She slept in dirty, airless huts with snakes, bats, fleas and mosquitos as her companions. She hunted antelopes, gazelles, lions and hyenas. She removed and preserved their skins and sent them back to the museum.

Her ultimate goal had been to live for a few months with a Pygmy tribe. Westerners knew little about these people, who were small in stature compared to them and most other Africans. The average height of most Pygmies was four feet, but there were men and women only three feet tall. A few were over five feet.

Their average weight was about 85 pounds.

Delia had been with the Bambute Pygmies in the Ituri Forest for two months now. They lived in leaf-thatched huts. Their mattresses, made of leaves and dried animal skins, rested on the ground near the fire. They covered their genitals with pieces of bark, cloth, or bunches of flowers or leaves. They wore no other clothing, but the men wore wooden whistles on lanyards around their necks.

The Pygmies did not grow food to eat. Instead the women gathered food—edible roots, leaves, caterpillars, lizards, snails and slugs. They took their babies on these gathering expeditions, cradled on their hips. The men hunted monkeys, birds, squirrels, elephants and okapis, a rare species of the giraffe family. Vine traps, with weighted poisoned spears at the top and poisoned stakes at the bottom, were stretched all along the jungle paths. Unlike white hunters, the Pygmies killed only for food, not for sport.

When Delia had first arrived, the villagers greeted her with equal amounts of suspicion and curiosity. The suspicion was gone, but she was still an object of curiosity. They had never seen a white woman before. Her pale skin and sapphire eyes fascinated the women. And her long white hair shocked them, for their hair didn't turn white until they were near death.

Even after two months everyone was still trying to find out whether her body was the same color as her hands and face. Rolling up her sleeves and showing her bare arms hadn't satisfied them. They wanted her to take off her clothing. Over and over she had refused, but they still persisted in trying to find out what was the true color of the skin of the "woman-with-an-old-head-on-a-young-body." Most evenings when she stepped into her rubber tub to bathe, she shooed away onlookers, men and women.

The bread was not yet cooled when she heard a faint birdlike whistle that signaled a hunt.

Six men suddenly appeared and gathered freshly poisoned spears from the trees, where they had hidden them from the children. Delia often hunted with the men and was curious to see what this hunt would bring. She put the bread in her tent and picked up her gun and ammunition. She put some permanganate tablets in her blouse pocket in case she needed an antidote to snakebites.

She followed the men into the bush. Within a half hour, they came across fresh elephant droppings. They mixed mud with the manure and smeared the mixture over their heads and bodies to disguise their own body odors. The tips of elephants' trunks can pick up the faintest aroma in the air, even from five miles away. And their large ears hear the slightest jungle sound—a rustling in the bush, the snapping of a twig.

Men from a nearby village appeared. They conversed in pantomime, fearful that even a whisper might be heard by the elephant. From their gestures, Delia concluded that a wounded elephant had escaped from a trap. The men would not rest until they found the elephant. It could take a few hours, a day, or several days. In open country elephants were fairly easy targets, but in the jungle the odds were in their favor. They moved easily through the dense and tangled vegetation. At twilight their straight round legs and wrinkled hides blended into the surroundings and were easily mistaken for tree trunks.

The chase would be exciting and exhausting. Delia didn't know whether she was up to it. She asked to be guided back to the village. No one would do it. She knew she couldn't find her way back through the bush alone. She fell in line behind the men.

After an hour or so they came to a stream banked on one side by maidenhair ferns and on the other by clusters of lilies. Scents of other unseen flowers filled the air. In the ground were deep holes—elephant footprints. The men examined the giant prints, crushed leaves and broken twigs to figure out which way the elephant had gone.

The trail led deeper into the jungle. Twisted growths of trees up to 160 feet high formed one continuous canopy overhead, blocking out the light. Under this umbrella the air was stifling and humid. The vegetation was so dense, Delia couldn't see clearly in any direction. Her body dripped with perspiration. She cautiously lifted branch after branch, trying to move as silently as the men did, but it was impossible for her to do so. They were used to the underbrush and vines. They maneuvered so gracefully through its tangles that not as much as a twig snapped under their bare feet.

A thorn caught in her long-sleeved shirt. The leader heard the tiny noise it made and angrily motioned for her to take off what she was wearing and hunt in the nude as they did. She gently refused.

They reached an open glade where chimpanzees sunbathed on rocks. A hunter drew his bow. Delia unintentionally bumped against him, and the arrow whizzed over the chimpanzee's head. Her companions shrieked at her in anger as the apes hightailed it into the dense bush.

The sound of splashing water interrupted

their tirade. The men gestured to each other about what to do next. One man suggested climbing a tree to see better. Another offered to investigate alone in the direction of the sound. The leader shook his spear and the discussion ended abruptly.

The path led to a swamp. The men, who weighed thirty pounds less than Delia, crossed without effort. But with Delia's first steps she sank ankle deep into a morass of dead leaves and green slime. Thousands of mosquitoes and black flies, resting in the oozy mud, rose like black clouds. A deafening buzz pierced the silence of the jungle. Delia felt herself sinking farther down. She grasped some brush to steady herself. The black clouds multiplied and thickened. The bites came fast and furious. In a few seconds the insects covered her face and neck and hands and arms. It was pointless to try to brush them off, for they would immediately be replaced by others.

She managed to pull herself out of the swamp onto dry land, but needle-sharp pains from the bites continued. Now red blotches covered her skin. The damp air felt suffocating. The men paid no attention to her, for their ears were again drawn to the sound of splashing water.

The leader crouched down. Delia stared over his head. Through an opening in the trees she saw thousands of huge butterflies with colorful wings lining the banks of a stream. Tiny birds with long tail feathers darted in and out of the foliage. Three purplish-brown bodies with striped legs and giraffelike heads were drinking in the stream. Delia stared at the okapis. She had never seen a live one before. Few white people had.

The okapis stamped their feet. The butterflies rose like a fluttering rainbow. The stamping stopped and the butterflies returned to the bank. Parrots flew out of the trees to a vine just over the animals' heads, then strutted back and forth on the vine. The beauty of the scene distracted Delia from her pain. But it did not distract the men from getting meat for their families.

Three hunters raised their spears. The

mother okapi lifted her creamy-white head as if startled. Her pointed ears bent forward. She nudged her calf out of the water. The butterflies rose and for a few seconds almost shielded the animals from the hunters' gaze. The spears shot through the air. The father fell. The mother and newborn vanished into the forest just as the other spears landed where they had stood.

The men rushed forward and encircled the dead animal. Its dark-purplish coat shone like satin. The okapi looked larger than any specimen Delia had seen in European museums— if only she could preserve the skin and bring it back to the States. But Delia knew no one would go back to the village to get the salt needed to cure the skin.

She looked at her watch. It was two o'clock. They had been in the bush for almost seven hours.

One of the men blew a whistle. A nest of sticks and leaves was created in the crotch of a fifteen-foot tree close to their prize. Two men climbed the tree to guard the meat until others from the village came to take the animal back.

The needle-sharp pains returned. Delia dove into the stream to seek refuge from the stinging bites. She dissolved permanganate tablets in her cupped hands and rubbed the mixture over her swollen face and arms. But the water and the rubbing made the itching even worse. She tried rubbing some undissolved tablets directly on her skin. It burned even more.

She flung her gun down on the ground and threw herself down on the banks of the stream. Almost immediately the huge butterflies covered her whole body. She watched them rise and flutter and then settle down again on her. Out of the corner of her eye she saw two bright eyes staring at her from the trees. Then two black faces fringed in white. The butterfly ballet continued. The black faces moved farther out of the trees, revealing themselves as monkeys. Delia laughed.

"Ssst." One of the men signaled that they

were moving on. She picked up her gun, wondering where she would get the stamina to continue.

They reached another muddy stream. Delia gave her gun to one of the men as he and the others quickly crossed a natural bridge made of vines. She stepped cautiously on the twisted cable, grasping overhead vines. Suddenly a trumpeting scream pierced the forest. Timber crashed. The men vanished into the bush. Delia was frozen in place. She saw the heads and backs of elephants crashing through the forest, like army tanks, tearing down vines and felling trees. She reached for her gun before realizing that she didn't have it. The shrill noise stopped, and so did the movement. The stillness was more frightening, for Delia knew that the elephants were getting ready to charge again.

The brush in front of her rustled, then parted. She saw a large head, then an elephant's body. The animal was at least 12 feet tall and must have weighed several tons. He was no more than a dozen yards from her.

His ears spread to their full 12-foot span and he waved his trunk from side to side. She didn't dare move or breathe.

The elephant unfurled his trunk and tipped it in Delia's direction. It was so close that she could see the red insides of its nostrils. She held her breath. If the elephant spotted her or smelled her, it might pick her up with its trunk and pound her to a pulp on the tip of his tusk. The elephant swept back its ears, rolled its trunk upward, then backed slowly into the bush. When Delia felt sure that the danger had passed, she whistled and the Pygmies returned.

A little farther on they came to the elephant. He was dead. Four poisoned spears and a poisoned bamboo stake from the vine trap had pierced his body. The men threw down their weapons and embraced each other. Two men blew repeatedly on their whistles. The others screeched with joy as they danced around the elephant.

They pulled out the spears, then carefully cut off the eyelashes and bits of the trunk and ear hair for good-luck charms. The tail hairs would be traded for palm wine to neighbors who wove them into jewelry.

As the sun moved lower in the sky, the men began eating the elephant meat. Delia collected wood for a fire. She was damp and uncomfortable in her thin, ragged shirt and mud-stained trousers. Darkness descended, and with it a cold mist and eerie sounds. Bats and huge beetles circled overhead. Bullfrogs croaked as loud as bass drums. Ants swarmed near the fire and the fresh meat. The men offered her meat. Delia hadn't eaten since breakfast, but she felt too exhausted to do so.

The men cleaned out the elephant's insides and continued feasting. When they were through, they crawled inside the elephant's hide to sleep. Delia lay down on the ground. She tried to sleep, but she felt edgy. The lack of food and her need for sleep made her un-characteristically afraid. She didn't want to be alone. She threw sticks at the elephant's hide to keep the men awake. When there was no response, she screamed that she had seen a leopard. The men came back to the fire and sat with spears in their hands until daylight.

By daylight the camp was filled with people from nearby villages who came to join the celebration. The Pygmies decorated their bodies with bark and flowers and leaves and painted patterns on their skin with clay and soot mixed with fat. The hunters reenacted the drama of the hunt for an appreciative audience. Palm wine and banana beer accompanied the abundance of meat. For five days Delia celebrated and feasted along with the community.

⁂

Delia left the Ituri Forest shortly after the hunt. She continued traveling through Africa looking for other peoples to photograph and hoping to find more specimens of Congo game. Sometime in July she contracted a fever. She recuperated, but after two more relapses decided it was time to go home. She had been traveling for almost eleven months.

Delia brought back numerous artifacts and over thirty animal specimens for the Brooklyn Museum. She wrote books describing her African experiences. In 1929 she went on a second expedition for the Brooklyn Museum. At sixty-four she remarried and retired. She died in 1970, at age ninety-five.

THE DEEP

March 18, 1959
Little Salt Springs, Florida

Eugenie Clark turned off her car motor. There was no point in trying to drive any farther. The morning's rain had turned the dirt road into mud. The rain wasn't going to stop in the next few hours either. But neither rain nor mud was going to stop her from diving into Florida's Little Salt Springs.

Eugenie had loved the water since she was two years old. In the summers her mother took her frequently to the beach or to a pool. The little girl had raced eagerly into the salty waves of the Atlantic Ocean and just as happily stepped into the calm waters of a pool. Ocean salt or pool chlorine didn't stop her from opening her eyes when she swam. She *had* to keep her eyes open: There was always the possibility of seeing something underwater—a pebble in the sand, the drain of the pool, or just her feet. Eugenie became a good swimmer by watching good swimmers, like her mother, her grandmother and her uncle. Her Japanese mother had once been a swimming teacher.

One Saturday when she was nine, Eugenie discovered the best swimmers of all. On her way to work, her mother left her to wander for a few hours among the big tanks of pale-green water and moving creatures at the New York Aquarium. When her mother picked her up to take her to lunch, Eugenie was filled with stories of what she had seen. Over *sashimi*—raw fish—and other Japanese delicacies, she told her mother about the fish that glowed like fire and the ones that shone like the moon. She described how swiftly some fish darted back and forth in the tanks while others lumbered their way along the bottom. She began to identify and distinguish these moving creatures on what became weekly trips to the Aquarium.

Her mother bought her a fifteen-gallon aquarium. She filled it with a rainbow—black-speckled red platies, pale-green swordtails, iridescent pearl danios and a white-banded red clown fish. Soon there was a second tank, and a third, and a terrarium. There were toads and snakes.

Eugenie observed the fish mating and spawning. She kept detailed records on what she saw. Her interest in fish grew as her aquarium and her records grew. She became the youngest person ever accepted into the Queens County Aquarium Society.

In college she studied to become an ichthyologist—a zoologist who specializes in studying fish. She became an expert diver, for there was no substitute for swimming alongside fish and observing sea life close at hand. She had gone on dives in Micronesia, Hawaii, the West

Indies, the Pacific and the Gulf of Mexico, and had spent a year studying marine life, especially poisonous fish, in the Red Sea. She had collected over 300 specimens. Now, at thirty-seven, she was the head of the Cape Haze Marine Laboratory in Florida, where she studied shark behavior as well as other marine life.

But today's dive wasn't to study fish. Bill Royal, a retired lieutenant colonel from the Air Force and a superior diver, had convinced Eugenie to dive with him in the cold, muddy, waters of Little Salt Springs. Royal had discovered a cave of stalactites 70 feet down in the springs. On a ledge above the cave he had found fossilized parts of skulls and other human bones. On a recent dive together with him, Eugenie had found more human bones and a large vertebra of an alligator.

Stalactites are formed over centuries in caves that are above water level; dripping water deposits minerals on the cave ceiling in ever-lengthening iciclelike formations. A geologist had confirmed that Florida's water level hadn't been low enough to produce the stalactites for at least 6,000 years. An anthropologist had speculated that the bones might be those of the prehistoric Indians who had built mounds found in many parts of Florida. Royal thought that maybe the bones belonged to the first humans who lived in caves when Florida's water level was lower. To find out if their assumption was correct, they needed more bone samples.

Eugenie got out of her car and carried her diving gear into a jeep with Royal and Bill Stephens, an underwater photographer. Stephens managed to drive a bit farther, but then his jeep got stuck. Eugenie put her air tanks on her back and carried her other equipment in her arms. She walked the next 50 yards through even softer mud. She came to the wooden planks on the ground that she and Royal had placed there on their previous trip. The planks were covered with mud. She stepped on one, slipped, sank up to her knees in mud and kept walking.

When they reached the rim of the springs, they found the other two members of the expedition already there. Charlie Corneal was putting a fiberglass boat into the water. Bud Kraft was testing the air tanks. He would stay at 100 feet with an extra tank of air in case anyone needed it. Eugenie, Royal and Stephens planned to buddy dive, staying close to each other.

Eugenie put her diving gear on a spot of dry land higher up and changed into her diving outfit—a long-sleeved T-shirt and jeans with tights under them. She wore woolen socks and sneakers under her flippers to keep her feet warm.

Cold is a problem for divers. The farther down they dive, the lower the temperature of the water becomes, and their bodies lose heat. When body temperature falls below 95° F (35° C), divers may be susceptible to amnesia. Today most divers wear wet suits to insulate their bodies, but in 1959, wet suits were not readily available.

She put four pounds of weights around her waist to ease her descent. Then she fastened her double air tank and regulator and stepped into the boat.

They rowed out to the deep part of the spring. Little Salt Springs is about 250 feet in diameter. It slopes down to about 60 feet, then drops into a hole 70 feet wide. Eugenie, Royal and Stephens planned to dive all the way down to the bottom, although they had no idea how far down the bottom really was. They were hoping to find missing parts of the skulls at the bottom.

Corneal dropped a rope off the side of the

boat. Royal dropped into the water first and started down on the rope. Eugenie went next, then Stephens, then Kraft.

They moved down easily to 20 feet, then to 30 feet. Eugenie could hardly see anything around her. Most Florida springs have such clear water, fish can be seen through the bottom of a fiberglass boat. But Little Salt Springs was so muddy, hardly anything could be seen in it.

Eugenie waited for her eyes to adjust to the dark, then she descended farther. At 60 feet she felt the ledge near the cave, but she couldn't see the cave. Deeper—70, 80, 90 feet. She could hardly see the beams of light coming from Royal's and Stephens's flashlights.

Suddenly Royal swam quickly up to the surface. Eugenie and Stephens thought something was wrong with him. They started swimming up. But before they got very far, Royal reappeared with a flashlight, which he handed to Eugenie.

They dove down again. At 80 feet the

waters were cold but manageable. Eugenie breathed easily with the help of her aqualung. At sea level air pressure is about 14.7 pounds per square inch. Every 33 feet down adds the same amount of pressure on the body. Human lungs and sinuses have difficulty with changes in air pressure. Some people's ears begin to hurt when they are only 10 feet below sea level.

At 80 feet Eugenie cleared her ears easily. She relieved the pressure by swallowing, then holding her mask close to her nose and gently blowing to equalize the pressure. Things were going so easily, she wasn't aware how far down she was.

As she swam farther down, she kept pointing the light ahead on Royal and occasionally turning it up onto Stephens. At 130 feet Stephens swam over to her. He pointed for her to show him her wrist gauge. She looked at the gauge with him. She couldn't decipher the numbers. She had no idea how deep they were, and she really didn't care. She illuminated her face with her light. Then she flashed it on Stephens's face, then Royal's. They looked as happy as she felt.

She dove still farther down. A wonderful sensation came over her. It was the air. She was breathing the freshest air she had ever breathed. It was just flowing into her mouth and into her lungs. It was rushing in so fast, it was hard to stop it. It was hard to exhale.

Suddenly the mud around her was so thick, even her light couldn't get through it. Where was Royal? She refocused the light and caught his hand on the rope. The fresh air was coming in more slowly now but it felt just as wonderful. Everything seemed slower, even her thinking.

She sank slowly into mud. It felt wonderful. She looked in the direction of her beam of light. She couldn't see Royal anymore. Where had he disappeared to? She saw a hand sticking up out of the mud and holding the rope. The mud danced in the light but the hand didn't move.

She focused her mind. Whose hand was it? Why was it motionless? Suddenly she knew.

It was Royal's hand and he was dead. She felt sad but calm. The realization that he was dead wasn't upsetting. She reached out to touch his hand. She remembered a man at a funeral reaching out to touch the corpse in the open coffin. But she couldn't reach Royal. She couldn't get to his hand.

Oh, how she wanted to sleep. She needed sleep. She was having a baby. The slow rhythm of her breathing turned into a voice. "Take a deep breath and we'll all go together now," it said. "Take a deep breath," the voice ordered her again.

Some feeling jarred her away from her thoughts. Something was wrong. *I'm not having a baby,* she realized. *I'm diving. I'm diving and I'm becoming anesthetized.* The nitrogen in the compressed air had affected her mind. She was experiencing "rapture of the deep." When nitrogen narcosis happens, divers get giddy and can't think straight.

She turned her head up, looking for Stephens. He wasn't there. *Where is he?* She felt dizzy. She had an impulse to take her mask off, but instead she pressed her hand over her mouthpiece. *I must not take it off.* She felt her mind floating. *No, I mustn't.* Slowly she began to focus her thoughts. *Don't take out the mouthpiece. If you do, you'll die.*

She kept her hand pressed on the face mask. With the other hand she grasped the rope. *Don't let go. Get up, get up.* She beat her flippers to help her ascent. She feared she would pass out. But she kept climbing with the light in her right hand.

Up, up, until the rhythm subsided and the feeling that she was taking in those deep wonderful breaths passed. She flashed her light around again. It was muddy and black. She still couldn't see Stephens. But she couldn't believe he would have left the rope without telling her. It was too dangerous.

The rope was her lifeline. She clutched it even tighter. She flashed her light around. Nothing but more mud and darkness. She refocused the light on the rope. Now it wasn't vertical. How could she get up if it didn't go up? Which side should she follow?

She remembered Royal once telling her what to do if she was ever so confused that she couldn't tell the direction of the rope. "Take off your weight belt," he had said. "Hold it out in front of you, and if it hangs upward, swim down to reach the surface."

She wrapped her legs around the rope and was just about to take off the weight belt, but instead felt for the bubbles coming out of her regulator. They were going off to her left. She crawled hand over hand in the direction of the bubbles, which had to be up.

As she ascended, she began worrying about Royal. *Where is he? Why was his hand so motionless? Is he stuck in the mud?* She couldn't go up without finding out if he was all right.

She changed direction and crept slowly down the rope hand over hand. She had no idea of how far down she was when she realized she might become hypnotized again. She might fantasize taking in those long, wonderful breaths of fresh air. Only this time she might not be able to stop herself from taking out her mouthpiece. She had to get out of the water now. She swam up the rope as quickly as she could. She felt terrible about abandoning Royal, but she knew she had to get up.

When she reached the less muddy part of the waters, she saw someone hanging on to the rope. She flashed her light on him. It was a man with a face mask. But it wasn't Royal or Stephens. *Who is this man?* It didn't matter. She was safe now. She was about to ask him who he was when she remembered. It had to be Kraft.

She signaled him that she was going up. She pointed down, hoping he would understand that Royal was still down there.

She swam up, past the cave of stalactites. Her eyes, adjusted from the black of the mud below, saw more clearly now. She swam up past the ledge. Up, up, until she saw the bottom of the boat. Then she surfaced.

Stephens was in the water near the boat. "I got nitrogen narcosis," she told him.

"So did I," he said. There was blood on his face and in his face mask. Stephens had come up so fast that the change in pressure had broken a blood vessel.

"I think Royal's in trouble too," she told Corneal. Corneal got ready to dive down when Royal and Kraft surfaced.

Everyone got into the boat. When they reached the shore, Corneal made a fire. Eugenie warmed her cold, shaking body. She felt relieved that Royal had never been in danger. He had just dived so far down into the soft sediment that he had disappeared from view. Royal thought he had gone down as far as 200 feet.

They drank hot tea and laughed, exhilarated that the adventure was safely over. After resting awhile, they got back into the boat to dive again.

Eugenie and the other divers found more bones that day. Royal found an entire human skeleton. Kraft found a fossilized antler whose side branches had been carved off, obviously by a human.

Eugenie and Royal continued their search for prehistoric human specimens. They dove in Warm Mineral Springs and found a partly burned three-foot log and human finger bones close by the log. Tests confirmed that the log was 10,000 years old.

They thought the bones might be 10,000 years old too. If so, they were the oldest human remains in the Western Hemisphere.

On a later dive, Royal found a human skull with the brain still in it; Eugenie believed it to be thousands of years old. Some scientists laughed at the idea that soft brain tissue could be preserved in water. Other scientists were convinced the story was a hoax.

Eugenie and Royal kept looking for scientific confirmation that the brain was ancient. Several years later a method of radiocarbon dating was developed. The finger bones and brain were tested and found to be at least 7,000 years old.

Today Eugenie Clark teaches zoology at the University of Maryland and is still an active diver.

GOING THE
DISTANCE

November 4, 1990
New York City
☙〰❧

Thecla Mitchell sipped coffee and looked out
her mother's kitchen window. She could see
a sliver of the pitch-black sky.

"I think we should get moving," said her
sister Terry, getting up from the kitchen table.
It was five forty A.M. The 26.2-mile New York
City Marathon was starting in twenty minutes.
It was only a five-minute ride to the starting
line on the Staten Island side of the Verrazano
Bridge, but Thecla had a reputation for being
late. Her sister didn't want to take any chances
this morning.

"Let's do it," Thecla answered. She was eager to start the race.

"I'll bring the van to the front." Thecla's childhood friend Patty picked up the car keys. Patty was looking forward to this marathon even more than the two mini marathons that Thecla had raced in, but she wasn't looking forward to driving Thecla's van. The van had been specially designed for Thecla.

Thecla was born a triple amputee: She had only a left arm. Both of her legs were missing above the knee, the left leg almost at the hip. But that hadn't stopped Thecla from driving—or doing almost anything.

She drove her van with hand controls. Her good left hand steered the van. She wore a special acrylic socket, held on by a shoulder harness on her right stump. This socket, attached to a long lever arm, allowed her to operate the gas and brake pedals using her right stump instead of feet. She pulled her arm back to accelerate and pushed it forward to stop.

The specially equipped van still had foot

pedals, and Patty would use them, but the hand controls always got in the way of her legs, making driving very awkward for her.

"Got everything?" said Thecla's mother as she opened the front door of the apartment.

"Everything but the vest, Ma," said Thecla, grinning widely.

It was November. Mrs. Mitchell had knitted Thecla a sleeveless wool vest to keep her warm, but today's temperatures were expected to reach the mid-70s. Thecla was wearing a short-sleeved T-shirt, her "good luck" shorts and light-blue pants over them.

"You'll use it in next year's marathon," her mother said, hugging her. Thecla loved and admired her mother. At birth thirty-three years before, Thecla was so weak and severely disabled that doctors in the hospital suggested that her parents put her in an institution. But Ruth Mitchell wouldn't hear of it. She saw the brightness in her baby's eyes and felt confident that Thecla was intelligent: Her daughter could have and deserved to have as normal a life as possible.

Her husband, Donald Greig Mitchell, agreed with her. He felt responsible for Thecla's disability. She had been conceived when he was undergoing chemotherapy for cancer; he felt sure the powerful effects of the treatment had altered the genes he had passed on to Thecla. The doctors assured him there was no way to know if this was true, but he remained convinced. He died eleven months after Thecla was born, and Ruth Mitchell raised her four children—Vivian, fifteen; Terry, eleven; Donald, three; and infant Thecla—alone.

Baby Thecla didn't have much strength, so she couldn't cry very loud. But Penny, the dog, heard her cries and awakened Mrs. Mitchell at night when Thecla needed her. At nine months, Thecla started talking and crawling and climbing stairs. She put her left arm and leg stump in front of her and propelled herself forward.

When Thecla went to first grade, she was fitted for prostheses for both legs and her right arm. She hated the artificial limbs. In those days they were heavy and difficult to use. She couldn't climb stairs or walk quickly wearing the legs, and they were impossible for playing sports. Thecla wore the prostheses only during school hours. She crawled the rest of the time.

Crawling was perfect for the basketball court. Her friends lowered the basket and she easily dunked shots into it with her left arm. She preferred sitting on a dolly when she played hockey. She always played defense; she stationed herself at goal, her stick in her left hand, and kept the opposing team members from scoring.

Thecla's close-knit family and friends buffered her from the taunts and shocked silences of outsiders when they saw the little girl with no legs and only a left arm crawling or wheeling around on a dolly. But even her family thought her childhood dream of being a veterinarian was impractical, and gradually she gave up the idea.

At ten Thecla had an operation to correct her scoliosis, or curvature of the spine. But the metal rods inserted in her back to straighten out the spine put pressure on her nerves and damaged her spinal cord. She became partially paralyzed. She lost sensation in her back. She also lost range of motion and power in her left shoulder and arm.

For two years she couldn't do anything but lie in bed. It was too painful to sit up for very long. She was so weak, recovering took all her energy. It was horrible going from being so active to being inactive and dependent on others to do everything for her. She vowed she'd never trust doctors again. She recovered gradually, but there was still some permanent damage to her motor control and nervous system. She never used the artificial legs again; she couldn't maneuver them.

The operation so debilitated her that for the next six years she had to be tutored at home. Her lack of traditional instruction ill prepared her for the rigors of a college education. She had a difficult time her first year at Long Island University. She graduated from college but didn't do well enough on the law boards to qualify for law school. It was the first time in Thecla's life that she felt truly handicapped. But instead of dwelling on this, she became a paralegal and now works for the New York State Attorney General's office in Manhattan.

It was still pitch-black out when Patty brought the van around. She pressed the toggle switches on the driver's door. The van door opened and a lift slid out. Thecla wheeled her chair onto it and pressed another set of controls on the lift, and the lift swung her up and into the van. Terry opened the front door and climbed into the passenger seat.

"Are you sure you have everything?" Patty asked.

"Yup. Let's go," Thecla said impatiently.

"What about your helmet?" asked Terry.

"Got it." Thecla had reluctantly agreed to wear a helmet. The able-bodied marathoners would start four and three quarters of an hour after she did, but since they were faster, they would eventually catch up. With thousands of runners jockeying for space, the streets

would be jammed. It would be easy for someone's foot to get caught in a wheel or for a
runner to dart out in front of Thecla, neces-
sitating a fast stop that could throw her out
of the chair. That plus New York's innumer-
able potholes and rocks in the streets made
wheelchair racing a dangerous sport. The helmet would protect her head from injury if she
fell.

Thecla reached into her sack and pulled
out the prosthesis that had been specially
made for her right arm so that she could use
both arms to wheel her new chair. First she
rolled a silicone suction piece onto her stump.
Around its top was a cloth to protect her skin
against irritation. A screw attached to the bottom locked it into a hard outer shell, which
ended in an inverted U-shaped curve. This
shape, rather like the grip of a hand, fit over
the right wheel on her chair, enabling her to
push it. She wrapped friction tape around the
bottom to give her an even better grip on the
wheel. She would wear a bicycle glove on her
left hand to protect it from the chafing and

irritation that were inevitable after turning the left wheel for 26.2 miles.

"We're almost there," Patty announced. Thecla's heart began racing as she looked out at the bridge lights illuminating the black sky. She locked her racing chair to stabilize it, leaned on it with her left hand and slid her body onto it. The chair weighed only twenty pounds, thirty pounds less than her regular chair, and as exhausting as it was going to be to wheel this chair for 26.2 miles, it would have been impossible with the heavier chair.

Ten months before, in December, Thecla had gone to a self-help support group for amputees led by a below-the-knee amputee and nurse, Paddy Rossbach, who headed the Research Amputee Rehabilitation Program at The Hospital for Special Surgery. Thecla asked about the rehabilitation program, and Paddy asked her if she had ever tried to wear artificial legs. They set up another meeting to talk.

At this meeting Thecla described the years of wearing artificial limbs and her painful recuperation from the scoliosis operation. Paddy explained how lightweight and flexible modern limbs were and showed Thecla the prosthesis for her left leg. She explained that it would be necessary for Thecla to be checked out at a series of clinics before embarking on such an ambitious program—limb fitting and exercise. Thecla was more than willing to do this even though she still harbored hatred for doctors.

She began preparing her body to support artificial legs. She was put on a diet to lose weight. She struggled and lost ten pounds, but she still needed to lose more.

Three times a week she got up at four thirty in the morning and drove into Manhattan for a ninety-minute workout at six o'clock. She needed to strengthen her muscles and improve her aerobic capacity, so her body could work harder but more efficiently. For thirty minutes she would work on an upper-body ergometer, turning the pedals with her left arm. For the next sixty minutes she did muscle-strengthening exercises specially designed for her, sit-ups to strengthen her abdominal muscles, and exercises to strengthen her right limb and both arms. The first time, after doing only ten sit-ups and five minutes of leg exercises, she was tired and felt her muscles straining. By the week before the marathon she had done sixty sit-ups and a full ninety-minute workout.

By March she had decided she wanted to race in the New York City Marathon. Thecla had always wanted to compete in the city's biggest athletic event of the year, but she had never been in good-enough shape before. Paddy encouraged her. An accomplished marathoner, Paddy had run in seven marathons and held the course record for a female amputee in the New York City (5 hours, 2 minutes) and London (4 hours, 52 minutes) marathons.

Thecla started going out on Tuesday evenings in Manhattan's Central Park with members of the Achilles Track Club. Founded in 1983 by Dick Traum, an above-the-knee amputee, this international running organization for runners with disabilities has forty chapters.

The first time out Thecla was exhausted after only a quarter of a mile. But she wasn't discouraged. She knew that with time and work all athletes build up their endurance. The second time her arms still ached, but she did a mile. Gradually Thecla could wheel the chair for five miles. By September she had run eight miles, by October fifteen miles. Last week she had run twenty miles. A writer who had walked with Thecla as she trained in the Park had quit after five miles. "I think I know which one of us is disabled," the writer had joked. She hailed a taxi and went home to recuperate.

In May Thecla had felt confident enough to enter a 5-kilometer race in Huntington, Long Island. In September she had participated in another 5-kilometer race in Westchester. That same month she had also competed in the National Amputee Championships in Ohio. She won gold medals in the shotput, the discus and the 5-K run. She won a silver medal for the 100-yard dash and a bronze medal for volleyball. Thecla loved winning.

The van pulled to a halt. "Uh-oh," said Patty. "We're on the wrong side of the bridge."

"What do you mean?" asked Thecla.

"There's a barrier here, and there's no way to cross it."

"C'mon. Just go through it," Thecla said. "What time is it anyway?" she asked anxiously.

Terry looked at her watch. "About ten to six."

"Oh, boy." Thecla laughed nervously. "Paddy's gonna kill me. She says I'm always late."

"You *are*," said Terry.

"I'll find someone to help us." Patty parked the van and disappeared into the dark. Five minutes later she returned, having extracted permission from a reluctant highway official to drive across the lower ramp to the other side of the bridge.

On the other side, fifty members of the Achilles Track Club were already lined up at the beginning of the bridge. Another fifty disabled runners, expected to make faster time, were starting at eight o'clock. The able-bodied marathoners would start at ten fifty.

Thecla wheeled to the starting line past disabled runners from countries all over the world—New Zealand, Russia, Mongolia, Norway, Trinidad, Poland, Tobago and Puerto Rico. There were blind runners, a deaf and blind runner, single and double amputees with artificial legs, amputees who ran with crutches, a woman with multiple sclerosis, a man with cystic fibrosis and a man with cerebral palsy who wheeled backward going up hills. She recognized a few faces from workouts and from the two mini marathons.

Paddy was there with Janet Nelson and Joan Carney. Most disabled runners had volunteers who ran part of or the whole race with them. Janet would accompany Thecla throughout. Joan, who had helped Thecla with her training runs, was taking the first sixteen miles. Paddy had intended to go the whole way with Thecla, but she was recovering from recent surgery on her left leg, and though she was wearing her prosthesis, she was not allowed to put any weight on it. She would run the three miles of the bridge with Thecla, then catch up with her the last eleven miles in Manhattan—all on crutches.

Using the van, Terry and Patty would wait for Thecla at twenty-minute intervals (assuming she ran twenty-minute miles) on the eleven-mile route in Brooklyn, cheering her on. They planned to be available for all 26 miles, but it would be more difficult in Manhattan. By that time the able-bodied marathoners would have caught up with Thecla and the streets would be packed.

"So you finally got here?" Paddy teased.

"Piece of cake." Thecla always joked to brush off her lateness.

An Achilles organizer walking along the line stopped at Thecla. "Aren't you going to be strapped in?" Her voice was strident.

"No," answered Thecla.

The woman continued to insist that it was too dangerous for Thecla to race unless she was strapped in. Thecla ignored her. She thought being strapped in was more danger-

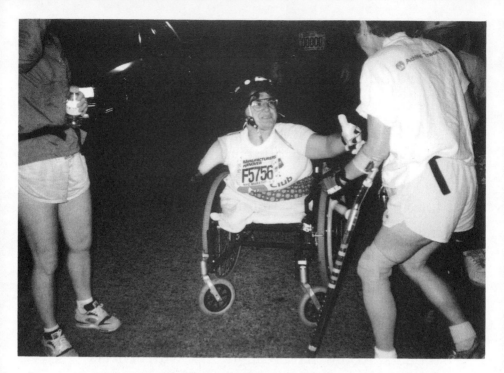

ous. It made her unable to maneuver and shift her weight to adjust to the many bumps and cracks in the road. And if the chair was pushed over, she'd be trapped under the weight.

"If you're in a wheelchair," the voice of another Achilles organizeer boomed through a megaphone, "please remember to go over the grates on the bridge slowly and at a forty-five-degree angle. The grates haven't been covered yet. They're very wide and easy to get caught in."

Thecla's chest constricted. *How do you breathe?* she thought. The darkness was lifting, and she could see the steep incline of the first mile on the bridge. It looked like a mountain.

"How do you feel?" Paddy asked.

"Okay, if I can only remember how to breathe." She put on her helmet. She was short of breath again.

"Okay, let's go," the Achilles organizer called out.

Thecla started wheeling up the incline. The blue sky was streaked with reds and pinks. The air felt crisp. *What a beautiful morning.* Her breathing was regular again. Her concentration returned. She started turning the wheels. *Nice, easy, smooth turns. There's no rush.* All of a sudden the incline didn't seem so big.

She overheard a volunteer for another runner instructing Paddy in how Thecla might more effectively wheel the chair. "Leave my athlete alone," Paddy interrupted the man in mid-sentence.

Thecla turned the wheels faster. *I am an athlete, and it feels great.*

All along the route spectators cheered Thecla on. She was overwhelmed at how many people called out to her by name. They had seen her interviewed on television two days before. Able-bodied runners turned around, clapping as they passed, calling out words of encouragement. At 120th Street and Fifth Avenue a man in the crowd called out, "God will bless you, baby." Without breaking her stride, Thecla said, "I think he already has."

About three miles from the finish line, Thecla felt dizzy. Her head ached, and so did her right side from a muscle pull. But she didn't tell her volunteers. Instead she told herself: *Calm down, relax, just get through it.*

Less than a mile from the end of the race, the sounds of the organ from the park carousel mixed with the roar of the crowd. At Central Park South, at the bottom of a steep hill, Thecla turned the wheel and her chair sped down the hill. Joan and Janet raced after her. (Joan Carney, who had intended to do only the first sixteen miles, was so moved by the crowd's responses to Thecla and to Thecla's spirit that she went the whole distance.) On crutches, Paddy couldn't catch up

with Thecla until the road became level again.

At three thirty P.M. Thecla crossed the finish line eight hours and fifteen minutes after she started. A silver-foil cape (given for warmth to all runners who complete the course) was thrown over her. At that moment the pain in her side disappeared. Her head was still aching, but she was so elated that it didn't matter. As proud as she felt of herself, she emphasized that she couldn't have made it without the loving support of her volunteers.

The next morning she went to her workout and went swimming. Her muscles were stiff, and she needed to warm them up.

After the marathon Thecla continued training to prepare for her artificial legs. On January 9, 1991, Thecla walked on her artificial legs for the first time. Once she is comfortable with them, she will take additional courses to prepare her to qualify for veterinary school.

❧ AFTERWORD ❧

These stories were reconstructed from first-hand accounts written by the women and from newspaper and magazine articles. Thoughts and dialogue were not fictionalized for the purposes of this book, but were taken directly from the adventurers' firsthand accounts and newspaper stories. The story about Bessie Coleman is the exception, as she left no firsthand accounts of her life.

The Birthday Party

In her short biography, *Over the Falls*, Annie Edson Taylor described the trip. Dwight

Whalen's biography, *The Lady Who Conquered Niagara*, was invaluable in providing background information about Annie's life, including the fact that she had lied about her age. Local newspapers covered the story in great detail. Donald Loker, Local History Specialist, Niagara Falls Public Library, lent his expertise to scrutinizing the text.

The Mountain that Refused to Be Climbed

Annie Smith Peck detailed her triumph over Huascarán in her book *A Search for the Apex of America.*

The Hunt

Delia Akeley described the elephant hunt in her book *Jungle Portraits.* Unfortunately, she never specified the exact date of the hunt. Elizabeth Fagg-Olds helped me pinpoint April as the month of the hunt.

Bird-in-Flight

Memoirs of the Late Bessie Coleman, by Elsie Patterson (Coleman's sister) and Anita King's articles in *Essence*, provided most of the biographical data for this story. Patterson described this particular exhibition in detail, but did not specify the date, except to say it was in the autumn. Based on other events in Bessie's life, I surmised it took place in 1923. Patterson noted the boy's question to Bessie. King's article included the letter from the girl to Bessie. Richard Duncan's book *Stunt Flying* was invaluable in explaining the various stunts. Renée Cafiero, Dom Pisano and Russell Lee scrutinized the text for accuracy of the mechanics of flying.

The Deep

Eugenie Clark recounted this adventure in the first of her two autobiographies, *Lady with a Spear*. Dr. Clark read the story for accuracy.

Going the Distance

Thecla Mitchell, her sister Terry Wilson, her friend Patty Reilly-Butcher and Paddy Rossbach shared the story of Thecla's life. I went on one of Thecla's training runs in the park,

and during the Marathon I crossed the Verrazano Bridge with her, then followed her in
the van with Terry and Patty throughout
Brooklyn and Queens to 71st Street and First
Avenue in Manhattan. The three of us agreed
to meet at the finish line at five thirty but
Thecla beat us there by two hours.

❧ APPENDIX ❧
WOMEN
ADVENTURERS

Here is a partial list of women adventurers:

Harriet Chalmer Adams (1875–1937) Explorer, writer, organizer and first president of the Society of Women Geographers

Delia J. Akeley (1875–1970) Hunter, explorer

Mary Lee Jobe Akeley (1876–1966) Explorer, photographer

Louise Arner Boyd (1887–1972) Leader of Arctic scientific expeditions

Fanny Bullock Workman (1859–1925) Mountain climber, explorer

Dr. Eugenie Clark (1922–) Ichthyologist, diver

Jacqueline Cochran (1910–1980) Aviatrix, cofounder of Women Airforce Service Pilots (WASP)

Bessie Coleman (1893–1926) First licensed black pilot in the world

Amelia Earhart (1897–1937) First woman to

cross the Atlantic Ocean in an airplane

Dr. Sylvia Earle (1935–) Marine scientist, diver, underwater explorer

Anna L. Fisher (1949–) Physician, expert in X-ray crystallography, astronaut

Marguerita Harrison (1879–1967) Newspaper correspondent

Christa McAuliffe (1948–1986) Teacher who was trained for the 1986 Challenger mission.

Ynes Mexia (1870–1938) Botanical collector, discoverer of over 500 new species

Thecla Mitchell (1957–) Marathon runner

Matilde Moisant (? –1964) Second licensed woman pilot in the United States

Shirley Muldowney (1940–) Race-car driver

Annie Smith Peck (1850–1935) Classicist, mountain climber

Harriet Quimby (1892–1912) First licensed woman pilot in the United States

Judith Resnick (1949–1986) Electrical engineer, astronaut

Sally Ride (1951–) Astrophysicist, astronaut

Blanche Stuart Scott (1890–1970) First American woman to make a solo flight

Kathryn D. Sullivan (1951–) Geophysicist, astronaut

❧ SELECTED ❧ BIBLIOGRAPHY

Akeley, Delia J. *The Biography of an African Monkey.* New York: Macmillan, 1929.

———. *Jungle Portraits.* New York: Macmillan, 1930.

Clark, Eugenie. *The Lady and the Sharks.* New York: Harper & Row, 1969.

———. *Lady with a Spear.* New York: Harper & Row, 1965.

Duncan, Richard. *Stunt Flying.* Chicago: Wilcox Company, Inc., 1930.

Fagg-Olds, Elizabeth. *Women of the Four Winds: The Adventures of Four of America's First Women Explorers.* Boston: Houghton Mifflin, 1985.

King, Anita. "Brave Bessie: First Black Pilot." *Essence*, May 1976, June 1976.

Moolman, Valerie, and the editors of Time-Life Books. *Women Aloft*. Alexandria, Va: Time-Life Books, 1981.

Patterson, Eloise. *Memoirs of the Late Bessie Coleman*. (Unpublished, 1969.)

Peavy, Linda, and Ursula Smith. *Women Who Changed Things*. New York: Scribner's, 1984.

Peck, Annie Smith. *Flying over South America: Twenty Thousand Miles by Air*. Boston: Houghton Mifflin, 1932.

————. *A Search for the Apex of America: High Mountain Climbing in Peru and Bolivia, Including the Conquest of Huascarán, with Some Observations on the Country and People Below*. New York: Dodd, Mead, 1911.

————. *The South American Tour*. New York: George H. Doran, 1913.

Taylor, Annie Edson. *Over the Falls: How the Horseshoe Falls Was Conquered*. Self-published by the author, 1902.

Whalen, Dwight. *The Lady Who Conquered Niagara*. Brewer, Maine: EGA Books, 1990.

Periodicals consulted for the story about Annie Edson Taylor were *The Bay City Times Press*, *Buffalo Evening News*, *The Daily Cataract-Journal*, *Niagara Falls Gazette*, *Niagara Falls Journal*.

PICTURE CAPTIONS
❧ AND CREDITS ☙